What Is Dancing For, Papa?

BY DR. INTERGALACTIC

EDITS BY ALYSSA HARDEN

PICTURES BY VISOEALE

AD ASTRA MEDIA, LLC • VIRGINIA

www.adastrasteammedia.com

ISBN: 978-1-0878-9297-9

IMPRINT: INDEPENDENTLY PUBLISHED

Copyright © 2021 Ad Astra Media, LLC. All rights reserved. Independently published in the United States by Ad Astra Media, LLC and Jose Morey.

What is dancing for papa?
What does it do?

Dancing is for me
And dancing is for you!

Dancing is for all of us
Each and every one

Whether you are English, Irish, Native, Chinese, or Bulgarian

Dancing is for smiling, for exercise, and to celebrate winning
You can dance by jumping or by spin- spin- spinning!

Dance is for fun
For any daughter or son

Dancing is for when you are feeling blue
You can do it in your bare feet
or with fancy shoes

Dancing can be for celebration
You can do it at home or on any occasion

Dancing can come at the end
of an adventure or at the start
Dancing can heal and even mend
a broken heart

You can dance to say sorry
or to show appreciation
You can dance in your car, at school,
or at work in any civilization

Dancing can help you learn math
and give you a strong body
Dancing can be for work or just a fun hobby

Dances can be hard to learn
and take a lot of work
But if you just want to have fun,
you can let yourself go berserk!

Dancing is for everyone,
it's something we all do
Dancing is for little boys
– and for grown men, too

There are ballet dancers who are women and ballet dancers who are men
Some fall somewhere in between — let me tell you again:

Dancing is a window into your true self
Whether it be himself, herself, or themself

Dancing is for all, no matter skill or age
Dancing is for brave warriors and for kids performing onstage

Dancing is for soldiers, doctors, and kings
Dancing can be done when it's quiet
or while someone sings

Some dances are fancy like mambos and tangos

Some dances are goofy and can be done while eating mangos

"Does it have to be mangos, momma?"
No, silly, it can be phalsa
But when you eat that, I want to see you dance the salsa!

Everyone all over the world knows
how to dance
It goes beyond language in any circumstance

Some dances are old, even ancient
They were done for worship and entertainment

So now I ask you, little one,
What is dancing for, what does it do?

Dancing is for little boys like me, papa
And dancing is for you

Dancing is the way I talk
and that which is most true
Dancing is from my heart and
how I say I love you

Dancing is for me

Ad Astra Media, LLC is a Latino owned S.T.E.A.M. media and edutainment company seeking to renew a faith in facts and reason and uplift underserved and minority communities by providing them with scientific role models in science, technology, engineering, art and math (S.T.E.A.M.) to which they can aspire. We are composed of individuals with experience at all levels of T.V. and commercial media production, running from traditional television services on Spanish and English networks all the way to leading streaming services and film studios. We have memorandums of understanding with digital animation studios supported by the Space Foundation and who have worked with Disney and Pixar.

See the full collections of the diverse multilingual S.T.E.A.M. children's series by Dr. Intergalactic,

Good Night Little Astronaut

What are tears for momma?

Good Night Little Doctor

Good Night Little Astronomer

Good Night Little Veterinarian

Good Night Little Engineer

Good Night Little Environmental Scientist

What Is Dancing For, Papa?

www.ingramcontent.com/pod-product-compliance
Lightning Source LLC
LaVergne TN
LVHW070256080526
838200LV00091B/360